The month of March, from the illuminated manuscript *Les Trés Riches Heures du duc de Berry*

The Story of a Special Day
Volume 86

March

26

85th day of the year
(86th in leap years)
280 days remaining
until the end of the year.

by Michael Dobson

Timespinner
Press

Table of Contents

Cover: The Vietnam Veterans Memorial in Washington, DC, by Derek Baird — for the *Event of the Day*.

Robert Frost

March 26 Quotations

"The difference between an icicle and a ret-hot poker is really much slighter than the difference between truth and falsehood or sense and nonsense; yet it is much more immediately noticeable and much more universally noticed, because the body is more sensitive than the mind."

A. E. Housman, poet, born March 26, 1859

"The world is full of willing people; some willing to work, the rest willing to let them.

Robert Frost, poet, born March 26, 1874

"Marx teaches us to blame society for our failures. Freud teaches us to blame our parents, and astrology teaches us to blame the universe. The only place to look for blame is within: you didn't have the guts to bring up your full moon and live the life that was your potential."

Joseph Campbell, mythologist, born March 26, 1904

"The theatre is a place where one has time for the problems of people to whom one would show the door if they came to one's office for a job."

Tennessee Williams, playwright, born March 26, 1911

"All good work is done in defiance of management."

Bob Woodward, reporter, born March 26, 1943

"There are two kinds of truth: the truth that lights the way and the truth that warms the heart."

Raymond Chandler, mystery writer, died March 26, 1959

"People are wrong when they say that the opera isn't what it used to be. It is what it used to be — that's what's wrong with it!"

Noël Coward, playwright, died March 26, 1973

"The central conservative truth is that it is culture, not politics, that determines the success of a society. The central liberal truth is that politics can change a culture and save it from itself."

Daniel Patrick Moynihan, politician and academic, died March 26, 2003

Event of the Day

Groundbreaking for the Vietnam Veterans Memorial

Veterans point out a familiar name
at the Vietnam Veterans Memorial

In 1979, four years after the end of the Vietnam War, a wounded Vietnam veteran named Jan Scruggs, inspired by the film *The Deer Hunter*, established the Vietnam Veterans Memorial Fund, Inc., to establish a memorial to the veterans of that war, and raised $8.4 million. By Act of Congress in 1980, three acres near the Lincoln Memorial were set aside for the proposed monument, and the US National Park Service established a design competition with a prize of $50,000.

There were four criteria: the memorial was to be reflective and contemplative in character, harmonize with its surroundings, contain the names of those who had died in the conflict or who were still missing, and make no political statement about the war.

Over 1,400 proposed designs were rated by a jury of eight architects and sculptors. Each design was identified only by number, and each juror independently rated each submission. The winning design — chosen unanimously — was by Maya Ying Lin, a 21-year old Yale University architecture student from Ohio. Lin proposed a memorial consisting of two long walls sunk into the earth, with the names of every US serviceperson killed in action or classified as missing.

The design, like the war it commemorated, was immediately controversial. A Vietnam veteran named Thomas Carhart referred to the proposed memorial as a "black gash of shame and sorrow." Former US Navy Secretary Jim Webb said, "I never in my wildest dreams imagined such a nihilistic slab of stone." Public outcry against the design led to the Secretary of the Interior, James Watt, refusing to issue a building permit for the project. The design was variously compared to a ditch or a gravestone, and the "V" shape of the memorial accused of being a subliminal anti-war peace sign. Maya Lin was called a "gook" and the jurors accused of being Communists.

Not all veterans felt that way. Many felt that the stark design was a solemn, dignified tribute to those who had fallen in the war. To resolve the controversy, the National Capital Planning Commission decided to add a statue and an American flag nearby. The bronze statue, known as The Three Soldiers, was by Frederick Hart.

The Three Soldiers statue by Frederick Hart

Ground was broken March 26, 1982, and the memorial was dedicated on November 13, 1982. On opening day, thousands of Vietnam War veterans marched to the site. In spite of the controversy, public opinion shifted radically and the Vietnam Veterans Memorial quickly became one of the most visited memorials in the nation's capital. One veteran declared the memorial "the parade we never got."

The Memorial Wall originally contained 58,191 names. As additional information has been collected, more names have been added. As of May 2011, there were 58,272 names, of which about 1,200 are classified as missing. The Three Soldiers statue was unveiled on Veterans Day 1984. A third memorial was added in 1993: the Vietnam Women's Memorial, designed by

Glenna Goodacre. An additional memorial plaque was added in 2004 to honor veterans who died after the war as a direct result of injuries suffered in Vietnam.

Visitors began leaving items at the memorial as soon as it opened, and several thousand items are left there each year. The National Park Service collects, catalogs, and stores all nonperishable items. Some of the items left there include a Harley-Davidson motorcycle with license plate HERO, a full-size replica "tiger cage" of the type used to imprison American POWs in North Vietnam, and even a Medal of Honor. Some of these items were put on display in a Smithsonian exhibition that ran from 1992 to 2003. Five traveling replicas of the Wall have been created; they visit hundreds of small towns and cities nationwide each year. Fixed replicas are located in New Jersey and Kansas, and a memorial of similar design to honor soldiers who fell in Iraq and Afghanistan is located in Irvine, California.

The Vietnam Veterans Memorial is ranked tenth on the "List of America's Favorite Architecture" by the American Institute of Architects.

March 26 Holidays and Celebrations

Martyr's Day and Democracy Day (Mali)

On March 22, 1991, a protest against Mali head of state Moussa Traoré turned violent when the military assaulted the peaceful demonstrators. Around 300 demonstrators were killed. A group of military officers, appalled by the massacre, launched a coup. Traoré was deposed on March 26, 1991, tried, convicted, and sentenced to death, but pardoned as part of a process of national reconciliation and healing. On Martyr's Day, the government and public lay wreaths on the Martyr's Monument in Bamako.

National Nougat Day (United States)

In the United States, almost every day of the year is dedicated to a particular food. Sponsored by manufacturers, retailers, farmers, or simply fans, these days are often proclaimed by the President, Congress, state governors, or mayors. March 26 is National Nougat Day. Nougat is made from sugar or honey mixed with roasted nuts, whipped egg whites, and sometimes candied fruit, and is used as an ingredient in many types of candy bars.

Prince Kūhiō Day (Hawaii)

One of only two US holidays dedicated to royalty, Prince Kūhiō Day marks the birth of Prince Jonah Kūhiō Kalaniana'ole (March 26, 1871 — January 7, 1922), heir to the throne of the Kingdom of Hawai'i, and later territorial delegate to the United States Congress. Kuhio was the only person ever elected to Congress who had been born a royal. He was active in Hawaiian politics and helped create many of the institutions and policies of the territory (and later state).

Prince Kūhiō

স্বাধীনতা দিবস *Shadhinata Dibôsh* **Independence Day and National Day (Bangladesh)**

March 26 is celebrated as Independence Day in Bangladesh to commemorate the country's declaration of independence from Pakistan in 1971. A nine-month war that followed claimed nearly three million lives. The মুক্তি বাহিনী (Mukti Bahini) freedom fighters defeated the Pakistani army on December 16, which is celebrated as Victory Day, celebrated with parades, political speeches, fairs, and ceremonies, beginning with a thirty-one gun salute in the morning.

Purple Day for Epilepsy (Canada)

On March 26, Canadians are encouraged to wear something purple as a way to raise awareness of epilepsy.

Christian Feast Days

In *Western Christianity,* saints commemorated on November 5 include Emmanuel, Felicitas, Larissa, Ludger, and Margaret Clitherow.

In *Eastern Orthodox Christianity,* it is the Synaxis of the Archangel Gabriel and the Apodosis of the Annunciation. Commemorated saints include the Martyr Codratus, Hieromartyrs Theodore and Irenaeus, Martyrs Philemon and Domninus of Thessalonica, Saint Eutychius, Saint Malcus of Chalcis, Venerable Stephen the Confessor and Wonderworker, Saint Felix of Trier, Saint Govan, and Saint Mocheallóg. (These are celebrated on April 8 by "Old Calendarists.)

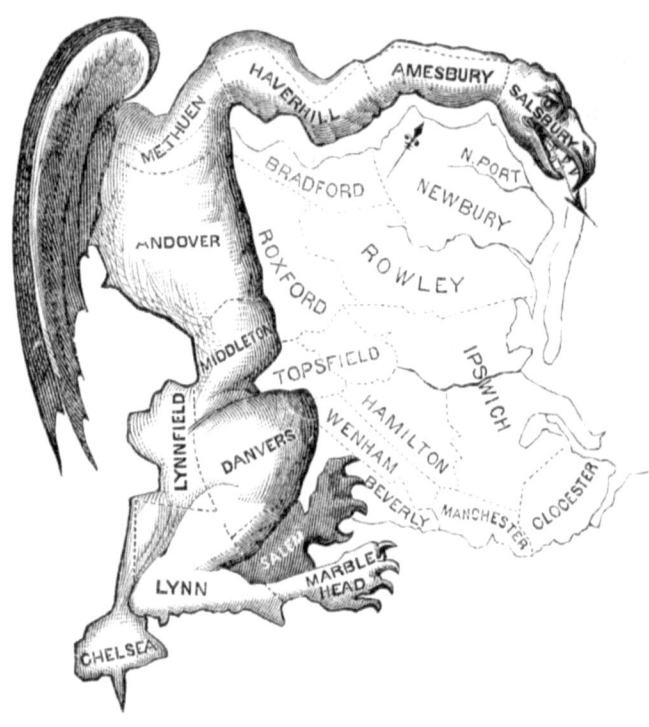

Original cartoon of "The Gerry-Mander," by Elkanah Tisdale,
published in the Boston *Centinel*, March 26, 1812

What Happened on March 26?

1344 – Siege of Algeciras Ends

As part of the Reconquest of Spain, Castillian forces laid siege to the Muslim city of Algeciras.. Begininng on August 3, 1342, and ending twenty-one months later on March 26, 1344, the siege forced the city to surrender, and it was incorporated into the Kingdom of Castille. Its historical importance is that it was one of the first military operations in Europe that used gunpowder.

1812 – "Gerrymander" Coined

When Massachusetts Governor Elbridge Gerry signed a bill to redistrict state senate districts to benefit the Democratic-Republican Party, one of the districts in the Boston area was so contorted that some people said it resembled a salamander. The redistricting was quite successful. Even though the Federalist Party won the House and the governorship, the carefully drawn districts ensured that the State Senate would stay in Democratic-Republican hands. While no one is sure who coined the word "gerrymander," a cartoon in the Boston Centinel by Elkanah Tisdale, first published on March 26, 1812, helped the word become a staple of the English language, used to this day.

1830 – The *Book of Mormon* is Published

The first edition of the Book of Mormon was published on March 26, 1830, by E. B. Grandin, a Palmyra, New York, printer. Joseph Smith, founder of the Church of Jesus Christ of Latter-Day Saints (Mormons), claimed to have found the text engraved on golden plates in a hitherto unknown version of "reformed Egyptian" and translated them. The building that included E. B. Grandin's bookstore has been restored and is now the Book of Mormon Historic Publication Site.

1958 – Explorer 3 Launched

On March 26, 1958, the United States launched its second successful satellite in the Explorer program. It lasted 93 days before its orbit decayed and it burned up on reentry on June 27, 1958. The Explorer satellites are most noted for their discovery of the Van Allen radiation belt that surrounds the Earth.

1979 – Egypt-Israel Peace Treaty Signed

On March 26, 1979, Egyptian president Anwar El Sadat and Israeli prime minister Menachem Begin signed the Egypt-Israel Peace Treaty, witnessed by US president Jimmy Carter. The treaty provided mutual diplomatic recognition, an end to the state of war that had existed officially between the two countries since 1948, the return of the Sinai Peninsula to Egypt, and the right of free passage of Israeli ships through the Suez Canal. As a result of this treaty, Egypt became the first Arab state to officially recognize Israel.

Handshake on the signing of the Egypt-Israel Peace Treaty, March 26, 1979. From left to right: Anwar El Sadat, Jimmy Carter, Menachem Begin

1997 – Heaven's Gate Suicides

The Heaven's Gate religious group believed that its members were aliens awaiting a spaceship that would be arriving with Comet Hale-Bopp. The planet Earth would be "recycled" and the only hope of survival was to leave immediately. By committing suicide, the souls of its members would be transmitted to the alien spacecraft. Begining on March 24, 1997, members of the group began to commit suicide, with the final suicides taking place on March 26, 1997, the same day the bodies were discovered.

1999 – Dr. Jack Kevorkian Charged

Pathologist Dr. Jack Kevorkian was a euthenasia activist who believed terminal patients had a right to die with the assistance of a physician, and claimed to have helped at least 130 patients commit suicide. Between 1994 and 1997, he was acquitted three times for assisting suicides. He was arrested and charged with second degree murder for the fourth time on March 26, 1999, and after a two-day trial was convicted of second-degree murder and sentenced to 10-25 years in prison. He was paroled in 2007 and died in 2011.

Who Was Born on March 26?

Arts and Fashion

T. Hee (March 26, 1911– October 30, 1988)

American animator Thornton Hee (always credited as "T. Hee") is best known for directing the "Dance of the Hours" segment of Walt Disney's *Fantasia,* and also worked for Leon Schlesinger Productions (Warner Brothers), UPA, and Terrytoons.

Guccio Gucci (March 26, 1881 – January 2, 1953)

Italian fashion designer and businessman Guccio Gucci founded the House of Gucci design firm.

Government, Law, and Military

Curtis Sliwa (March 26, 1954 –)

Activist Curtis Sliwa (right) founded the Guardian Angels, a group of self-appointed public safety guards who wore distinctive red berets. He is also a conservative radio talk show host.

Elaine Chao (March 26, 1953 –)

Former Secretary of Labor Elaine Chao (趙小蘭) was

the first Asian Pacific American woman and the first Chinese American to serve as a Cabinet official.

Bob Woodward (March 26, 1943 –)

Journalist Bob Woodward came to prominence along with his partner Carl Bernstein in reporting the Watergate scandal, co-authoring the 1974 best-seller *All the President's Men.*

Nancy Pelosi (March 26, 1940 –)

Nancy Pelosi was the 60th Speaker of the United States House of Representatives and the only woman to have held that role. To date, she is the highest-ranking female politician in US history.

Mahmoud Abbas (March 26, 1935 —)

Mahmoud Abbas (مَحْمُود عَبَّاس) served as the first Prime Minister of the Palestinian Authority. He was chairman of the Palestine Liberation Organization (PLO), and was also known as أَبُو مَازِن (Abu Mazen).

Sandra Day O'Connor (March 26, 1930 –)

Sandra Day O'Connor was the first woman appointed to the US Supreme Court, and served as an associate justice from 1981 to 2006.

Swearing in of Associate Supreme Court Justice Sandra Day O'Connor. From left to right: Chief Justice Warren Burger, husband John O'Connor, Sandra Day O'Connor

William Westmoreland (March 26, 1914 – July 18, 2005)

US General William Westmoreland commanded US military operations in Vietnam from 1964 to 1968 and subsequently served as US Army Chief of Staff. He was the subject of the CBS special *The Uncounted Enemy: A Vietnam Deception,* and sued CBS for libel, ultimately settling for an apology.

이승만 (Syngman Rhee) (March 26, 1875 – July 19, 1965)

Korean leader Syngman Rhee was the first president of South Korea. He was forced to resign in 1960 in the face of public protests against a disputed election, and he died in exile in Hawaii.

Letters

Erica Jong (March 26, 1942 –)

Author Erica Jong is best known for her first novel, 1973's *Fear of Flying*, which introduced the term "zipless f***."

Vine Deloria, Jr. (March 26, 1933 – November 13, 2005)

American Indian author and activist Vine Deloria, Jr. is known for his 1969 book *Custer Died for Your Sins: An Indian Manifesto*, which helped gain national attention for Native American issues.

Gregory Corso (March 26, 1930 – January 17, 2001)

Gregory Corso was one of the inner circle of Beat Generation writers along with Jack Kerouac, Allen Ginsberg, and William S. Burroughs. Abandoned and abused as a child, he was incarcerated in Clinton Prison in New York after a series of petty crimes, where he fell under the protection of Mafia boss Lucky Luciano. Self-educated, he started writing poetry. Allen Ginsberg saw some of his work, recognized his talent, and helped him become published. Corso was the subject of the documentary *Corso: The Last Beat*.

Tennessee Williams (March 26, 1911 – February 25, 1983)

Playwright Tennessee Williams is the author of such classics as *The Glass Menagerie*, *A Streetcar Named Desire*, and *Cat on a Hot Tin Roof*.

Tennessee Williams

Viktor Frankl (March 26, 1905 – September 2, 1997)

Holocaust survivor, neurologist, and psychiatrist Viktor Frankl wrote the 1959 English best-seller *Man's Search for Meaning: From Death Camp to Existentialism* (originally published in German in 1946 as *Trotzdem Ja Zum Leben Sagen: Ein Psychologe erlebt das Konzentrationslager*).

Joseph Campbell (March 26, 1904 – October 30, 1987)

Joseph Campbell was best known for his work in comparative mythology and comparative religion, including such books as *The Hero With a Thousand Faces* and *The Masks of God*. George Lucas credited *The Hero With a Thousand Faces* with shaping the story for *Star Wars* and Disney used the book in developing the script for *The Lion King*. Campbell was also the subject of the 1988 Bill Moyers documentary series *The Power of Myth*.

Robert Frost (March 26, 1874 – January 29, 1963)

American poet Robert Frost became one of the most popular and critically acclaimed twentieth century American poets, receiving four Pulitzer Prizes and a Congressional Gold Medal for his work. Perhaps his best known poem is "Stopping by Woods on a Snowy Evening" ("Whose woods these are / I think I know / His house is in the village, though...").

A. E. Housman (March 26, 1859 – April 30, 1936)

Poet and scholar A. E. Housman is best known for his poem cycle *A Shropshire Lad* ("When I was one-and-twenty / I heard a wise man say, / "Give crowns and pounds and guineas / But not your heart away...."

Charles Mackay (March 26, 1812 – December 24, 1889)

Scottish author Charles Mackay is best known for his book *Extraordinary Popular Delusions and the Madness of Crowds.*

Music

Kenny Chesney (March 26, 1968 –)

Country singer Kenny Chesney was chosen as the Country Music Association Entertainer of the Year in 2004, 2006, 2007, and 2008.

Charly McClain (March 26, 1956 –)

Country singer Charly McClain's hits include "Who's Cheatin' Who" and "Sleeping With the Radio On."

Teddy Pendergrass (March 26, 1950 – January 13, 2010)

Teddy Pendergrass was lead singer of Harold Melvin and the Blue Notes. Following an automobile accident that left him paralyzed from the chest down, he went on to a successful solo career.

Steven Tyler (March 26, 1948 –)

Steven Tyler, known as the "Demon of Screamin," is lead singer of the band Aerosmith. He is a member of the Rock and Roll Hall of Fame and the Songwriters Hall of Fame.

Diana Ross (March 26, 1944 –)

Singer Diana Ross (right) came to fame as lead singer of The Supremes, the most successful vocal group in US history, and in her subsequent solo career was named Female Entertainer of the Century by *Billboard* Magazine and the most successful female music artist in history by the *Guinness Book of World Records*. She was inducted into the Rock and Roll Hall of Fame in 1988.

Pierre Boulez (March 26, 1925 –)

French composer Pierre Boulez is known for his experimental compositions in twelve-tone technique, serialized music, controlled chance, and electronic music.

Performing Arts

Keira Knightley (March 26, 1985 –)

Keira Knightley first became well known for the 2002 film *Bend It Like Beckham* and for her role as Elizabeth Swann in the *Pirates of the Caribbean* film series, and has starred in such films as 2005's *Pride & Prejudice* and 2012's *Anna Karenina*.

The Supremes on the *Ed Sullivan Show*, 1966. From left to right: Florence Ballard, Mary Wilson, Diana Ross

Sarah Jean Underwood (March 26, 1984 –)

Sara Jean Underwood was *Playboy* Magazine's 2007 Playmate of the Year and a host of the TV series *Attack of the Show!*

Natalie Livingston (March 26, 1976 –)

Daytime actress Natalie Livingston won an Emmy for her role as Emily Quartermaine on *General Hospital* and also played on *Days of Our Lives*.

T. R. Knight (March 26, 1973 –)

Actor T. R. Knight played Dr. O'Malley on the ABC series *Grey's Anatomy*.

Leslie Mann (March 26, 1972 –)

Named "Hollywood's queen of comedy" by Elle magazine, Leslie Mann is known for her roles in such films as *The Cable Guy, The 40-Year-Old Virgin, Knocked Up,* and *17 Again*.

Michael Imperioli (March 26, 1966 –)

Michael Imperioli won an Emmy for his role as Christopher Moltisanti in *The Sopranos* and also appeared in the series *Law & Order*.

Eric Allan Kramer (March 26, 1962 –)

Eric Allan Kramer played Little John in the 1993 Mel Brooks film *Robin Hood: Men in Tights* and co-starred in the sitcom *The Hughleys*.

Billy Warlock (March 26, 1961 –)

Billy Warlock acted in the TV series Baywatch and in daytime shows *Days of Our Lives* and *General Hospital*.

Jennifer Grey (March 26, 1960 –)

Daughter of actor Joel Grey, Jennifer Grey starred in the films *Ferris Bueller's Day Off* and *Dirty Dancing,* receiving a Golden Globe nomination for the latter.

Leeza Gibbons (March 26, 1957 –)

Entertainment talk show host Leeza Gibbons became known as the co-host of the TV series *Entertainment Tonight.*

Martin Short (March 26, 1950 –)

Comedian Martin Short is known for his work on the television series *SCTV* and *Saturday Night Live.* He appeared in such films as *Three Amigos, Innerspace,* and *Mars Attacks!*

Ernest Lee Thomas (March 26, 1949 –)

Ernest Lee Thomas played Roger on the sitcom *What's Happening!!* and Mr. Omar on *Everybody Hates Chris.*

Vicki Lawrence (March 26, 1949 –)

Actress Vicki Lawrence is best known for her role on *The Carol Burnett Show* and its spin-off series *Mama's Family,* and for her 1972 hit song "The Night the Lights Went Out in Georgia."

"Went With the Wind" sketch, The Carol Burnett Show, 1977. From left to right: Carol Burnett, Vicki Lawrence, and Dinah Shore

Johnny Crawford (March 26, 1946 –)

Child star Johnny Crawford began as a member of the Mousketeeers before gaining the role of Chuck Connors' son in the TV series *The Rifleman.*

James Caan (March 26, 1940 –)

James Caan had leading roles in *The Godfather, Brian's Song, Misery, Kiss Me Goodbye,* and many other films.

Alan Arkin (March 26, 1934 –)

Actor and director Alan Arkin is known for his work in such films as *The Russians Are Coming, The Russians are Coming, Catch-22,* and *Glengarry Glenn Ross.* He won an Academy Award for Best Supporting Actor for his role in *Little Miss Sunshine.*

Leonard Nimoy (March 26, 1931 –)

Actor Leonard Nimoy (right) is best known for playing the role of Spock in the original *Star Trek* television series and its many spin-offs.

Bob Elliott (March 26, 1923 –)

Actor and comedian Bob Elliott was one-half of the comedy duo Bob and Ray, and is the father of comedian Chris Elliott.

Strother Martin (March 26, 1919 – August 1, 1980)

Character actor Strother Martin is best remembered as the warden in the film *Cool Hand Luke* who said, "What we've got here is a failure to communicate."

From left to right: Leonard Nimoy and William Shatner from the original *Star Trek* television series.

Sterling Hayden (March 26, 1916 – May 23, 1986)

Actor Sterling Hayden was a leading man in such films as *Johnny Guitar* and *The Asphalt Jungle,* and in later life became a character actor in such films as *Dr. Strangelove* and *The Godfather.*

Fred Karno (March 26, 1866 – September 18, 1941)

English theatre impressario Fred Karno is credited with inventing the custard-pie-in-the-face gag. He employed the young Charlie Chaplin and his understudy Arthur Jefferson. (Jefferson later took the name Stan Laurel.)

Science and Technology

Richard Dawkins (March 26, 1941 —)

Ethnologist and evolutionary biologist Richard Dawkins pioneered the gene-centered view of evolution and authored 1976's *The Selfish Gene* that introduced the term "meme." An outspoken atheist, Dawkins also wrote *The God Delusion.*

公文 公 (Toro Kumon) (March 26, 1914 — July 25, 1995)

Japanese mathematics educator Toro Kumon developed the Kumon method for teaching mathematics. He founded the Kumon Institute of Education to operate Kumon Centers worldwide. At any time, more than 4 million students study math using his methods.

Paul Erdős (March 26, 1913 — September 20, 1996)

Mathematician Paul Erdős was famous for his extensive body of collaborative work, and is one of the most prolific publishers of papers in the history of mathematics. The "Erdős number" is assigned to mathematicians based on their degree of separation from Erdős in collaborative papers: over 200,000 mathematicians worldwide have an Erdős number. He is the subject of the documentary film *N is a Number: A Portrait of Paul Erdős* and the book *The Man Who Loved Only Numbers*.

James Bryant Conant (March 26, 1893 — February 11, 1978)

Chemist James Conant began as a US Army chemist working on the development of poison gases. After the war, he joined the Harvard University faculty and became president of that institution, admitting women to the medical school and law school for the first time.

As a member of the National Defense Research Committee in World War II, he oversaw the development of synthetic rubber and helped oversee the Manhattan Project to build the first atomic bomb. Following his retirement from Harvard, he became United States High Commissioner for Germany and subsequently served as ambassador to Germany. Later in life, he became a noted critic of the educational system in the United States, publishing numerous books on the topic.

Othmar Ammann (March 26, 1879 — September 22, 1965)

Structural engineer Othmar Ammann designed and built more than half of the bridges that connect New York City to the mainland of the United States, including the George Washington Bridge, the Triborough Bridge, and the Verrazano Narrows Bridge.

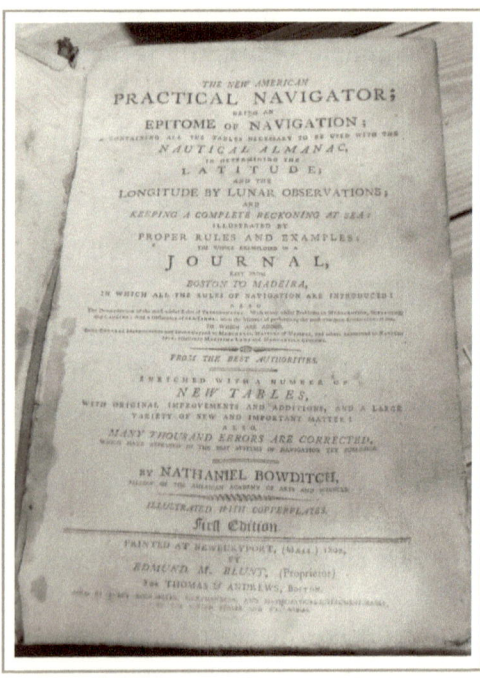

Nathaniel Bowditch (March 26, 1773 — March 16, 1838)

Mathematician Nathaniel Bowditch is considered the father of modern maritime navigation. Every commissioned U.S. Navy ship carries a copy of his book *The New American Practical Navigator,* often referred to simply as "Bowditch."

Above: Title page of the first edition of Nathaniel Bowditch's *The New American Practical Navigator,* 1802

Sports

John Stockton (March 26, 1962 –)

Utah Jazz point guard John Stockton was inducted into the Naismith Memorial Basketball Hall of Fame in 2009.

Marcus Allen (March 26, 1960 –)

Former football running back and CBS analyst Marcus Allen is a member of the College Football Hall of Fame and the Pro Football Hall of Fame.

Wayne Embry (March 26, 1937 —)

Basketball center/forward Wayne Embry played for the Cincinnati Royals, the Boston Celtics, and the Milwaukee Bucks, and subsequently became the first African-American NBA general manager. He was made a member of the Naismith Memorial Basketball Hall of Fame in 1999.

Portrait of Ludwig van Beethoven by Joseph Karl Stieler

Who Died on March 26?

Arts and Fashion

Halston (April 23, 1932 – March 26, 1990)

Fashion designer Roy Halston Frowick, known as Halston, came to fame for designing the pillbox hat worn by First Lady Jacqueline Kennedy to the 1961 Presidential Inauguration. Called by Newsweek "the premier fashion designer of all America," his clothes were worn by Bianca Jagger, Liza Minelli, Lauren Bacall, and Elizabeth Taylor. He was a pioneer in licensing, so his clothes were affordable by women at different income levels.

Government and Politics

Geraldine Ferraro (August 26, 1935 – March 26, 2011)

New York Congresswoman Geraldine Ferraro was the first female vice presidential candidate on a major American political party ticket as Walter Mondale's Democratic running mate in the 1984 US Presidential election.

James Callaghan (March 27, 1912 – March 26, 2005)

James Callaghan was prime minister of the United Kingdom from 1976 to 1979, and is the only politician in British history to have served in all four of the Great Offices of State: Prime Minister, Chancellor of the Exchequer, Home Secretary, and Foreign Secretary.

Daniel Patrick Moynihan (March 16, 1927 – March 26, 2003)

Sociologist and politician Moynihan was senator from New York, and held ambassadorial and other roles in four consecutive presidential administrations, from JFK to Gerald Ford. He was also known for his scholarly and popular books.

Daniel Patrick Moynihan

Edmund Muskie (March 28, 1914 – March 26, 1966)

Edmund Muskie was Governor of Maine (1955-1959), a US Senator (1959-1980), the Democratic nominee for Vice-President in 1968, a candidate for the Democratic Presidential nomination in 1972, and US Secretary of State from 1980 to 1981.

Senator Edmund Muskie (left), President Jimmy Carter (right)

Anthony Blunt (September 26, 1907 – March 26, 1983)

British art historian Anthony Blunt was publicly unmasked in 1979 as a member of the Cambridge Five, a group of British students (including Kim Philby) recruited to be Soviet spies in the 1930s.

During the Second World War he was a member of the British security service MI5, where he passed information decrypted from German codes to the Soviet Union. His spying was actually uncovered in 1963, and in return for his full confession, his spying career was kept secret for fifteen years and he was given immunity from prosecution.

David Lloyd-George (January 17, 1863 – March 26, 1945)

David Lloyd-George was prime minister of the United Kingdom from 1916 to 1922, leading Britain through the First World War and establishing the modern British welfare state.

Cecil Rhodes (July 5, 1853 – March 26, 1902)

Businessman and mining executive Cecil Rhodes was chairman of De Beers, the leading company in the diamond trade, which marketed 90% of the world's diamonds at its height. He founded the southern Africa territory of Rhodesia (now the countries of Zambia and Zimbabwe), and is considered the most important figure in South Africa in the 19th century. He founded the Rhodes Scholarships, which are funded by his estate.

Samuel Ward (May 25, 1725 – March 26, 1776)

Samuel Ward was a colonial governor of Rhode Island and a delegate to the Continental Congress, as well as a founder and trustee of Brown University.

John Winthrop (January 12, 1587/8* – March 26, 1649)

Puritan John Winthrop was governor of the Massachusetts Bay Colony for twelve of the colony's first twenty years of existence. (*See "On Names and Dates.")

John Winthrop

Letters

Diana Wynne Jones (August 16, 1934 – March 26, 2011)

Award-winning fantasy author Diana Wynne Jones is known for her young adult novels, including the *Chrestomanci* series and the *Dalemark Quartet.* She also wrote *Howl's Moving Castle,* made into the Academy Award-nominated 2004 film by Hayao Miyazaki.

Alex Comfort (February 10, 1920 – March 26, 2000)

Alex Comfort is best known for his 1972 work *The Joy of Sex.*

Roland Barthes (November 12, 1915 – March 26, 1980)

French literary theorist Roland Barthes was a pioneering figure in the development of a number of theoretical schools such as structuralism, semiotics, and post-structuralism.

林語堂 (Lin Yutang) (October 10, 1895 – March 26, 1976)

Chinese writer and translator Lin Yutang moved to the United States in the 1930s after his criticisms of the Nationalist government caused him to fear for his life.

In the United States, he became a best-selling author and a translator of classical Chinese works into English. As an inventor, he also developed the first Chinese-language typewriter.

Noël Coward (December 16, 1899 – March 26, 1973)

Playwright, composer, and actor Noël Coward's famous works include the plays *Present Laughter* and *Blithe Spirit* and songs such as "Mad About the Boy" and "Mad Dogs and Englishmen."

Raymond Chandler (July 23, 1888 – March 26, 1959)

Mystery novelist Raymond Chandler is famous for his books *The Big Sleep* (made into a 1946 film starring Humphrey Bogart as his character Philip Marlowe); *Farewell, My Lovely*; and *The Long Goodbye*. His prose style became known as "Chandlereque," for such turns of phrase as "Dead men are heavier than broken hearts."

Walt Whitman (May 31, 1819 – March 26, 1892)

Generally regarded as one of the most greatest and most influential poets in American history, Walt Whitman (next page) is most famous for his collection *Leaves of Grass*, which was highly controversial in its day for sexual imagery, especially in such poems as "I Sing the Body Electric." Considered a pioneer of free verse, he is also known as America's "poet of democracy."

Walt Whitman

Music

Eazy-E (September 7, 1963 – March 26, 1995)

Rapper Eric "Eazy-E" Wright was a member of the group N.W.A. and had a highly successful solo career, where he became known as the "Godfather of Gangsta Rap."

Eddie Lang (October 5, 1902 – March 26, 1933)

Eddie Lang was the first major jazz guitarist, playing with such musicians as Joe Venuti, Jean Goldkette, Frankie Trumbauer, Bix Beiderbecke, Paul Whiteman, Hoagy Carmichael, Bing Crosby and many others. He is in the Grammy Hall of Fame, the Big Band and Jazz Hall of Fame, and the ASCAP Jazz Wall of Fame.

Ludwig van Beethoven (December 17, 1770 [baptised] – March 26, 1827)

Universally considered one of the greatest composers of all time, Ludwig van Beethoven (page 34) is one of the "three Bs" (along with Bach and Brahms) that define classical music. Born in Germany, he moved to Vienna in 1792, gaining a reputation as a virtuoso pianist. His hearing began to fail in 1800, and he was almost totally deaf for the last years of his life. While he no longer conducted or performed in public, he created some of his most famous work while unable to hear it performed. He was buried in Vienna, with over 20,000 people attending his funeral procession.

Performing Arts

Jan Sterling (April 3, 1921 – March 26, 2004)

Jan Sterling won a Golden Globe and received an Academy Award nomination for her role in the 1954 film *The High and the Mighty,* and also appeared with Kirk Douglas in the 1951 film *Ace in the Hole.*

Sarah Bernhardt (October 22 or 23, 1844 – March 26, 1923)

French stage and screen actress Sarah Bernhardt, often referred to as the "Divine Sarah," is one of the most famous theatrical figures in the world. In addition to her work on the international stage and in early silent films, she was also a painter, sculptor, and author.

Sarah Bernhardt (Photo: Nadar)

Public Figures

Frank Searle (March 18, 1921 – March 26, 2005)

Photographer Frank Searle became famous for taking photographs purported to be of the Loch Ness Monster that were later revealed to be fakes.

Photograph of the Loch Ness Monster by Frank Searle

Science and Technology

David Packard (September 7, 1912 – March 26, 1996)

David Packard and his partner William Hewlett founded the technology company Hewlett-Packard in his garage in 1939 on an initial investment of $538. At the time of his death, his personal net worth was US $3.7 billion.

Joseph-Ignace Guillotin (May 28, 1738 – March 26, 1814)

Although the guillotine is named for Joseph-Ignace Guillotin, he did not actually invent the device (that honor goes to Antoine Louis) and in fact opposed the death penalty altogether.

His contribution came in the form of a speech before the French National Constituent Assembly (*Assemblée nationale constituante*) on October 10, 1789, in which he proposed that if there was to be capital punishment, that it should be by means of a painless decapitation, rather than the axe or sword, neither of which were reliably quick or painless, or hanging, which had the same problem.

Although a man named Guillotin was later executed by guillotine, it was not Joseph-Ignace or a relative of his. His family, embarrassed by their association with the guillotine, first petitioned the French government to rename the device, and when that failed, changed their own names.

James Hutton (June 14, 1726 [O.S. June 3, 1726*] – March 26, 1797)

Scottish geologist James Hutton developed the fundamental geological principle of uniformitarianism, and is known as the Father of Modern Geology for establishing geology as a formal science. (*See "On Names and Dates.")

Sports

Patricia McCormick (1929 – March 26, 2013)

Patricia McCormick was the first female American professional bullfighter in Mexico.

George Sisler (March 24, 1893 – March 26, 1973)

"Gentleman George" (also known as "Gorgeous George") Sisler (right) was a first baseman for the St. Louis Browns and the Washington Senators, and elected to the Baseball Hall of Fame in 1939. He played for the University of Michigan in college. He is listed by *The Sporting News* as one of baseball's 100 greatest players of all time.

The month of March, Alexander & Simon Bening
Brevarium Grimani,, fol. 4v

The Month of March

"Up from the sea, the wild north wind is blowing
Under the sky's gray arch;
Smiling I watch the shaken elm boughs, knowing
It is the wind of March."

> — "March," John Greenleaf Whittier

In ancient Rome, March was the first month of the year. As the first month of spring, in the Mediterranean climate it marked the beginning of the military campaign season. That's why March (Martius) is named in honor of Mars, the Roman god of war.

Although the first month of the year was moved back to January sometime during the transition of Rome from a kingdom to a republic (historians differ), March was the first month of the year in Russia until the end of the 15th Century, and is the first month of the year in many other cultures and religions.

In the northern hemisphere, March 1 marks the beginning of meteorological spring. In the southern hemisphere, March is the equivalent of September, making southern hemisphere March the beginning of autumn.

March is one of the seven months that have 31 days in it. March starts on the same day of the week as November every year, and except for leap years starts on the same day as February. March starts on the same day of the week as the previous June except for leap years, and in leap years starts on the same day as the previous September and December.

March in Other Cultures

The month of March has different names in different languages. Some nations use calendars other than the Gregorian, and their months may overlap with March.

- Arabic (Egypt, Sudan, Yemen): مارس (Māris)
- Chinese and Japanese: 三月
- Croatian: Ožujak
- Czech: Březen
- Finnish: Maaliskuu (earthy month).
- Greek: Μάρτιος
- Hebrew: מרץ
- Hindi: मार्च
- Korean: 3 월에 (3 wol-e)
- Old English: Hreþmōnaþ
- Polish: Marzec
- Russian: март
- Slovene: Sušec
- Ukranian: березень (birch tree)
- Vietnamese: 腸吧 (tháng ba)

March Superstitions

"Beware the Ides of March (March 15)!"

"March comes in like a lion and goes out like a lamb."

"April borrowed from March three days, and they were ill."

The first three days of March are unlucky "blind days." If rain falls on these days, farmers will have poor harvests.

Children born on Easter Day will be fortunate; children born on Good Friday are doomed to be unlucky.

"If Our Lord falls in Our Lady's lap/England will meet with a great mishap." (If Good Friday or Easter fall on Lady Day, March 25, the Feast of the Annunciation of Our Lady, national misfortune will befall.)

Clothes washed on Good Friday will never come clean.

Children should not climb trees on Good Friday.

Bread baked on Good Friday will never go moldy; eggs laid on Good Friday will no spoil.

Marriages that take place during Lent will have trouble.

"Married when March winds shrill and roar/Your home will be on a distant shore."

Good days to be married in March are March 3, 5, 13, 20, and 23. Which day? "Monday for wealth, Tuesday for health, Wednesday the best day of all, Thursday for losses, Friday for crosses, Saturday for no luck at all."

March Symbols

Birthstone
Aquamarine (left) and bloodstone, both representing faithfulness, courage, and friendship.

Birth Flowers
Daffodils (right), symbolizing rebirth and new beginning. Daffodils are also the 10th wedding anniversary flower.

March Events

Honorary Months

Presidents, Congresses, and nations around the world issue proclamations recognizing particular months to honor certain causes. These events generally fall in March. (All US unless otherwise noted.)

- National Nutrition Month
- American Red Cross Month
- Women's History Month (celebrated in Canada during October)
- Irish-American Heritage Month
- Colorectal Cancer Awareness Month
- Fire Prevention Month (The Philippines)

Women's Suffrage Demonstration 1917

"March Madness" (United States)

The NCAA Men's Division I Basketball Championship, popularly known as "March Madness" or the "Big Dance," is a single-elimination tournament to establish the champion college basketball team.

Moveable and Multi-Day Events

Some events take place over a specific week or time period. Start and finish dates may vary from year to year. Some events occur on different days each year (such as "fourth Saturday of a month").

Seward's Day (Alaska)

Seward's Day, on the last Monday in March, commemorates the signing of the Alaska Purchase Treaty on March 30, 1867. The earliest it can occur is March 25 and the latest is March 31.

Birkat Hachama (ברכת החמה) (Judaism)

According to the Talmud, the Sun was created at the vernal equinox position at the beginning of the Jewish month of Nisan, established by tradition as March 25 on the Julian calendar (see "On Names and Dates").

The Birkat Hachama, "Blessing of the Sun" is recited when the vernal equinox occurs at sundown on a Tuesday, which happens every 28 years. When the Julian calendar gave way to the Gregorian calendar in 1582, the date shifted forward, and continues to shift slowly forward by approximately a day per century.

Birkat Hachama took place on April 8, 2009 (14 Nisan 5769), and will occur next on April 8, 2037 (23 Nisan 5797).

Birkat Hachama at the Western Wall, 2009

Earth Hour (International)

On Earth Hour, held on the last Saturday of March each year, households and business are urged to turn off all non-essential lights for one hour between 8:30pm to 9:30pm on each person's local time. The goal is to raise awareness of the need to take action on climate change.

La crucifixion by El Greco

Easter Season

The Christian holiday of Easter in Western Christianity is held on the first Sunday after the Paschal Full Moon following the March equinox, which is officially set at March 21 by church reckoning. Easter itself can therefore occur as early as March 22 and as late as April 25, but occurs most often in April. In Eastern Christianity, which uses the Julian calendar, Easter occurs between April 4 and May 8. This also sets the date for the various events that lead up to Easter, most importantly the events of Holy Week. (For an explanation of Julian and Gregorian dates, see "On Names and Dates.")

Passion Sunday

The fifth Sunday of the Christian season of Lent is known as Passion Sunday in various Protestant denominations and by some traditionalist Catholics. Sometimes, the sixth Sunday of Lent is referred to as Passion Sunday, but it is more commonly known as Palm Sunday. Passion Sunday starts the two-week Passiontide, which ends on Holy Saturday, the day before Easter, commemorating the day that Jesus's body was laid in the tomb. The fifth Sunday of Lent can occur as early as March 8 (though the next time it will be that early is in 2285 CE), and as late as April 11.

Palm Sunday

The moveable feast of Palm Sunday commemorates the triumphant entry of Jesus into Jerusalem, an event mentioned in all four gospels. In many Christian churches, palm leaves are distributed to the worshippers. The earliest date for Palm Sunday is March 15, and the latest is April 18.

Maundy Thursday

The Thursday before Easter is Maundy Thursday, when the Last Supper took place. Because of its relation to Easter, the earliest day it can occur is March 19, and the latest it can occur is April 22.

Good Friday

Good Friday, observed during Holy Week on the Friday preceding Easter Sunday, commemorates the crucifixion of Jesus and his death at Calvary. Because of its relation to Easter, the earliest day it can occur is March 20, and the latest it can occur is April 23.

Holy Saturday

Sometimes called Easter Eve or Black Saturday, Holy Saturday commemorates the day in which Jesus's body lay in the tomb. Some mistakenly refer to this day as "Easter Saturday," but that properly describes the Saturday following Easter, the last day of Easter Week. The earliest it can occur is March 21, and the latest it can occur is April 24.

Easter

Easter celebrates the resurrection of Jesus Christ on the third day after his crucifixion. In the liturgical calendar, Easter follows the season of Lent, and begins the period known as Eastertide, which ends on Pentecost Sunday. Easter is observed religiously in a morning service. In the U.S., it's also common to decorate Easter eggs and make Easter baskets of eggs and candy, often with the Easter bunny as a symbol. The White House traditionally hosts an egg hunt, and many communities have Easter parades. Easter customs around the world include bonfires (Cyprus, western Sweden), men spanking women with a ceremonial whip (Czech Republic and Slovakia), egg fighting (Bulgaria), cross-country skiing and reading murder mysteries (Norway), and children dressed as witches collecting candy door-to-door (other Nordic countries).

Easter Eggs

Easter Monday

In some Roman Catholic and Eastern Orthodox cultures, the Monday after Easter is celebrated as a holiday. It is also known as Egg Nyte, featuring egg rolling competitions and dousing other people with water that had been blessed with holy water the previous day at mass. Easter Monday is also celebrated as Family Day in South Africa. In Guyana, people fly kites that were made on Holy Saturday. In Portugal, it is known as the Anjo (Ivy) Festival, in which people picnic in the countryside.

Śmigus-Dyngus (Poland, Hungary, Czech Republic, Slovakia)

The Monday after Easter in Poland and in the Polish diaspora is known as Śmigus-Dyngus, or simply Dyngus Day in the US. Boys throw water over girls they like and spank them with pussy willows. Girls avoid getting wet by giving boys "ransoms" of painted eggs.

Easter Week (Western Christianity), Bright Week (Eastern Christianity)

The period from Easter Sunday to the following Saturday is known as Easter Week. In both Western and Eastern Christianity (where it's known as Bright Week), the resurrection continues to be celebrated in church services. Easter Tuesday is a public holiday in the Australian state of Tasmania.

March Zodiac Signs

From the perspective of someone on Earth, the Sun appears to move through the sky throughout the year, along a path astronomers call the ecliptic plane. The ecliptic plane is divided into twelve constellations, known as the zodiac, based on traditionally observed patterns of stars. On your birthday, you can't see your constellation, because it's in the daytime sky.

The zodiac was first developed by Babylonian astronomers about 2,500 years ago. Because they were unaware that the Earth wobbles like a spinning top (known as precession), they didn't make allowance for the fact that the Sun's path through the zodiac changes over time.

That means there are now two sets of dates for your birth sign. The *tropical* dates are the original Babylonian dates; the *sidereal* dates tell you where the Sun actually appears as it moves along its annual path.

For March 26, the tropical sign is **Aries**, and the sidereal sign is **Pisces**.

Pisces

Tropical February 20 to March 20
Sidereal March 15 to April 14

In the Roman legend of Venus and her son Cupid, they escaped the clutches of Typhon, known as the "father of all monsters," by transforming into fish and tying themselves together with rope. That's why the name Pisces is plural for fish. The constellation appears as a somewhat ragged "V" shape, representing the rope, with the "fish" located at the two rope ends.

In astrology, Pisces is a water sign, compatible with the other water signs Cancer and Scorpio, as well as with the earth signs Taurus, Virgo, and Capricorn. Pisceans are supposed to be imaginative, compassionate, unworldly, secretive, and escapist.

Aries

Tropical March 21 to April 19
Sidereal April 15 to May 15

In Greek mythology, Aries is a ram with golden wings and golden wool who rescued the twins Phrixus and Helle from certain death. Although Helle died in the rescue attempt, the grateful Phrixus sacrificed the ram to Zeus. The golden fleece from the sacrificed ram played a prominent part in the later myth of Jason and the Argonauts.

In astrology, Aries, a fire sign, is compatible with the other fire signs of Gemini, Leo, and Sagittarius, and to a lesser extent with air signs Scorpio and Libra. Arians are supposed to be adventurous, enthusiastic, quick-tempered, and impulsive.

Illustration by Edward Penfield

What Day of the Week is March 26?

On what day of the week does March 26 fall?

Surprisingly, this isn't an easy question. Because the calendar year is 365 days long (366 in leap years), it doesn't divide evenly by the seven days of the week.

Also, the Earth goes around the Sun in about 365-1/4 days, so a calendar tends to drift over time. That's why the same date falls on different weekdays in different years.

This is made even more complicated by a change in calendars that took place in 1582. Our modern calendar has its roots in ancient Rome, in a calendar reform conducted by Julius Caesar. Caesar commissioned mathematicians to attack the problem, and they came up with the idea of leap years, and thus standardized the calendar for centuries to come. This was called the Julian calendar.

Over time, however, the small errors in Caesar's calculation compounded. That's why Pope Gregory XIII commissioned the Gregorian calendar, used in most of the world today. Some countries converted in 1582, when the calendar was first developed; some converted later; other still haven't changed.

Gregorian and Julian aren't the only types of calendars. The Hebrew year, the Islamic year, and many other calendars are used in different parts of the world and among different people.

You can convert Gregorian dates to other calendars, including the Hebrew calendar, the Islamic calendar, and even the Mayan calendar by visiting the Fourmilab Calendar Converter at http://www.fourmilab.ch/documents/calendar/.

Chinese calendar systems are quite complex and have changed several times; a full discussion is far beyond the scope of this book. If you're interested, you can find information here: http://www.hermetic.ch/cal_stud/chinese_cal.htm.

A 50-year brass perpetual calendar.

On Names and Dates

Historians use "CE" (Common Era) and "BCE" (Before the Common Era) instead of the more common "AD" (Anno Domini, or Year of Our Lord) and "BC" (Before Christ), reflecting the fact that the year-numbering system established by the Gregorian calendar is used throughout the world in many countries not culturally Christian.

The CE/BCE designation dates back to at least 1708, and has been adopted as a standard by the United Nations and the Universal Postal Union. Because this series of books covers events and people of all nations and cultures, we use the CE/BCE terms.

The abbreviation "O.S." ("Old Style") on some dates refers to the fact that the Russian Empire did not switch from the Julian to the Gregorian calendar at the same time as the rest of Europe, and therefore some figures and events have two dates.

Also, in the Julian calendar in England in the 16th century, the year began on March 25 rather than January 1. To avoid confusion with Gregorian dates, dates between January and March were often written using both years.

People and events whose original names are not in the Western alphabet have their native names (where possible) in the appropriate script shown in parenthesis. If you are using an e-reader to access an electronic version of this book, all characters don't always display on all devices.

Cartoon by John T. McCutcheon

Copyright, Credit, and Contact

Follow Us

Our blog Dobson's Improbable History (http://improbhistory.blogspot.com) features short articles on events and people associated with each day, and updates several times each week.

You can also get a daily "What Happened In History" message and all the latest Timespinner Press news by following us on Facebook at https://www.facebook.com/TimespinnerPress. Our Twitter feed @SidewiseThinker links you to all our News of the Day.

Contact Us

Find an error or a format problem? Want information about the series, about us, or about when the volume for your special day might be available? Please email us at editor@timespinnerpress.com. (We also take requests if your special day isn't yet complete. Please give us at least six weeks' notice if possible.)

Sources

We owe a great debt to Wikipedia, which is our first stop for research. We attempt to make independent confirmation of all important dates and facts through a variety of other sources. Other sources we frequently use include the Library of Congress; "on this day" listings from *Encyclopedia Britannica*, the New York *Times*, and the BBC; and, of course, the always essential Google.

All art and photographs are either in the public domain, used under a Creative Commons license, or with a "fair use" justification, and most frequently come from Wikimedia Commons and the Library of Congress Prints and Photographs Division.

Attribution is provided where possible, or as requested by the copyright owner, or when there is particular historical significance, listed below. For information about any particular illustration or photograph, please contact us.

Credits

- The cover photograph of the Vietnam Veterans Memorial was taken by William D. Moss in 2010. It is in the public domain as a work of the US Federal government.
- The illustration of the month of March is from the French Gothic illuminated manuscript on the back cover and in the frontispiece *Les Très Riches Heures du duc de Berry* by the Limbourg Brothers, Jean Colombe, and an intermediate painter whose name is lost to history. It is in the public domain because its copyright has expired.

- The 1961 photograph of Robert Frost was taken by New York *World-Telegram & Sun* photographer Walter Albertin. It is in the public domain because it is part of a collection donated by the New York *World-Telegram & Sun* to the Library of Congress. Per the deed of gift, all rights in these photographs were dedicated to the public.

- The photograph of US veterans at the Vietnam Veterans Memorial is in the public domain as an official photograph taken by the US Department of Defense. It carries the identification number 060911-D-7203T-030.

- The photograph of the Three Soldiers statue by Frederick Hart is in the public domain as an official photograph taken by Sgt. Michael J. Cardin of the US Department of Defense. It carries the identification number 100708-D-7377C-007a.

- The photograph of Prince Kuhio was taken in the 1890s and is in the public domain because its copyright has expired. The original photograph is in the Hawaii State Archives.

- The cartoon "The Gerry-Mander" by Elkanah Tisdale was published in the Boston *Centinel* in 1812. It is in the public domain because its copyright has expired.

- The photograph of the triple handshake among Jimmy Carter, Anwar El Sadat, and Menachem Begin was taken by a *U.S. News and World Report* photographer. It is in the public domain because it is part of a collection donated by *U.S. News and World Report* to the Library of Congress. Per the deed of gift, all rights in these photographs were dedicated to the public.

- The photograph of the title page of the first edition of Bowditch's *American Practical Navigator* was taken by Daderot and released into the public domain by the photographer. The original manuscript is in the Miami History Museum, and is in the public domain because its copyright has expired.

- The 2006 photograph of Curtis Sliwa was taken by Charles Kaiser and is used here under CC-BY-SA 2.0.

- The photograph of the swearing in of Associate Justice Sandra Day O'Connor is from the collection of the Ronald Reagan Library, part of the US National Archives and

Records Service. No known copyright restrictions on this image exist.

- The 1965 photograph of Tennessee Williams was taken by New York *World-Telegram & Sun* photographer Orland Fernandez. It is in the public domain because it is part of a collection donated by the New York *World-Telegram & Sun* to the Library of Congress. Per the deed of gift, all rights in these photographs were dedicated to the public.

- The 1966 publicity photograph of The Supremes on the *Ed Sullivan Show* is in the public domain because it was published in the United States between 1923 and 1977 without a copyright notice.

- The 1977 publicity photograph from *The Carol Burnett Show* is in the public domain because it was published in the United States between 1923 and 1977 without a copyright notice.

- The 1968 publicity photograph from *Star Trek* is in the public domain because it was published in the United States between 1923 and 1977 without a copyright notice.

- The 1976 photograph of Daniel Patrick Moynihan at a meeting of the Senate Foreign Relations Committee was taken by *U.S. News and World Report* photographer Marion S. Trikosko. It is in the public domain because it is part of a collection donated by *U.S. News and World Report* to the Library of Congress. Per the deed of gift, all rights in these photographs were dedicated to the public.

- The 1977 photograph of Senator Edmund Muskie and President Jimmy Carter was taken by a White House staff photographer, and is in the public domain as a work of the US Federal government. It is in the collection of the Jimmy Carter Library, National Archives and Records Administration.

- The painting of John Winthrop is by an unknown artist, dated around 1800, based on an original likeness probably painted in England before 1630. The original is in the collection of the US National Portrait Gallery, Smithsonian Institution, Washington, DC. It is in the public domain because its copyright has expired.

- The 1887 photograph of Walt Whitman is by George C. Cox, and is said to have been Whitman's favorite photograph. It was restored by Adam Cuerden in 1979. The original is in the collection of the Library of Congress. The photograph is in the public domain because its copyright has expired.

- The 1820 painting of Ludwig van Beethoven composing the *Missa Solemnis* is by Joseph Karl Stieler. The original is in the collection of the Beethoven-Haus in Bonn, Germany. The painting is in the public domain because its copyright has expired.

- The 1866 photograph of Sarah Bernhardt was taken by the pioneering French photographer Nadar (Gaspard-Félix Tournachon).

- The photograph of the Loch Ness Monster was taken by Frank Searle. The copyright status of the photograph is unknown, but is presumably copyrighted. It is used here under "fair use" provisions of the copyright law to illustrate a biographical entry on the photographer. Its resolution is too low to make it suitable for the production of counterfeit works and no comparable "free use" or public domain alternative exists.

- The 1914 photograph of George Sisler was cropped from a University of Michigan team portrait, originally published in the 1915 *Michiganensian*. The photographer is unknown. The original can be found in the collection of the Bentley Historical Library. The image is in the public domain because its copyright has expired.

- The plate März (March) is from the c.1510 *Brevarium Grimani* by Gerard Horenbout and Alexander and Simon Bening. It is in the public domain because its copyright has expired.

- The photograph of aquamarine has been released into the public domain.

- The photograph of daffodils is by Myrabella, and is licensed under the Creative Commons Attribution-Share Alike 3.0 Unported license.

- The 1917 Women's Suffrage demonstration comes from the Library of Congress, Prints and Photographs Division, LC-USZ62-31799 DLC, and is in the public domain because its copyright has expired.

- The 2009 photograph of Birkat Hachama at the Western Wall is by "Ingo," and is used here under CC-BY-SA 3.0.

- The painting *La crucifixión* by El Greco is located in the Museo del Prado. It is in the public domain because its copyright has expired.

- The photograph of Czechoslovakian Easter eggs was taken by Jan Kameníček, who has released the image into the public domain.

- The 50-year perpetual calendar photograph is in the public domain.

- The cartoon by John T. McCutcheon is from his 1905 collection *The Mysterious Stranger and Other Cartoons by John T. McCutcheon.* It is in the public domain because its copyright has expired.

- The painting of März (March) is from the calendar book *Festkalender* by Hans Thoma. It is in the pubic domain because its copyright has expired.

License Description and Terms

Aside from material purely in the public domain, photographs and other material in this book are used under specific licenses permitting free use, usually with an attribution requirement. For full text and terms of these licenses, click or enter the appropriate links below. If you believe there is an error in the copyright status or attribution of any of these images, please email us.

- Creative Commons Attribution 2.0 Generic (CC-BY 2.0): http://creativecommons.org/licenses/by/2.0/deed.en

- Creative Commons Attribution-Share Alike 3.0 Generic (CC-BY-SA 3.0): http://creativecommons.org/licenses/by-sa/3.0/

Timespinner
Press

The month of March, by Hans Thoma